LIVING WITH
DIABETES

Jenny Bryan

RSVP
RAINTREE
STECK-VAUGHN
PUBLISHERS
A Steck-Vaughn Company

Austin, Texas

Titles in the series
Living with Asthma
Living with Diabetes
Living with Down Syndrome
Living with Epilepsy

Published by Raintree Steck-Vaughn Publishers, an imprint of Steck-Vaughn Company

Library of Congress Cataloging-in-Publication Data
Bryan, Jenny.
Living with diabetes / Jenny Bryan.
    p.   cm.—(Living with)
    Includes bibliographical references and index.
    Summary: Discusses the causes, nature, and symptoms of diabetes, how it is affected by medicine and diet, and what to do in an emergency.
    ISBN 0-8172-5575-3
    1. Diabetes in children—Juvenile literature.
    [1. Diabetes. 2. Diseases.]
    I. Title.
    RJ420.D5B79   2000
    618.92'462—dc21   98-20105

Printed in Italy. Bound in the United States.
1 2 3 4 5 6 7 8 9 0 03 02 01 00 99

Picture acknowledgments
The publishers would like to thank The British Diabetic Association cover (top left), 7 (top), 20, 26, 27 (bottom), 29; Chapel Studios 12, 13, 23; Science Photo Library/Simon Fraser 9 (top), Science Photo Library/St. Bartholomew's Hospital 9 (bottom), Science Photo Library/Chris Priest & Mark Clarke 21, Science Photo Library/Mark Clarke 22 (top), Science Photo Library/Russell D. Curtis 22 (bottom); Tony Stone/Getty Images 28; Wayland Picture Library 7 (bottom), 8, 14, 15 (both), 27 (top).

All the other photographs were taken by Angela Hampton.

Most of the people who are photographed in this book are models.

The illustration on page 6 is by Michael Courtney.

Contents

Meet Julie, Tim, Mr. Hussain, and Charlie

Julie has had diabetes for as long as she can remember. She needs injections of insulin twice a day. Her mother used to give them to her, but now Julie gives them to herself. Sometimes she injects her leg, and sometimes she injects the insulin into her arm. She's very good at it now, and it doesn't hurt.

▽ Alan didn't know about diabetes until he met his friend Tim.

△ A timer on her computer reminds Julie to have her injections.

Alan was very worried when his friend, Tim, felt dizzy on the bus home from school. No one knew what to do. Alan knew that Tim had diabetes but didn't know that he needed a snack in the afternoon and had forgotten to eat it.

◁ Charlie loves sports, especially roller-blading, baseball, and tennis.

Charlie and his sister, Mai, were born in Hong Kong, but the family now lives in the United States. Charlie seems to get lots of attention because he has diabetes. Mai can't understand what all the fuss is about, because Charlie can do everything that other boys do.

△ Jemilla reminds her grandfather to take his pills every day.

Mr. Hussain has had diabetes since he was 50, and it has caused him other problems with his health. Sometimes his feet hurt, and he finds it painful to walk. So his granddaughter, Jemilla, carries things for him. Jemilla also goes to the hospital with her grandfather when he needs to see the doctor. She translates for him because he doesn't speak English very well.

What Is Diabetes?

We all need energy—not just when we are active but all the time—even when we are asleep. We get our energy from food. People who have diabetes are not able to turn the sugar from their food into energy.

If you have diabetes, your body does not have or cannot make the best use of a hormone called insulin. The body makes insulin in a gland called the pancreas, which is about 6 inches (15 cm) long and lies across the back of the stomach. Insulin is needed to use the sugar in the blood for energy. It also controls the level of sugar in the blood.

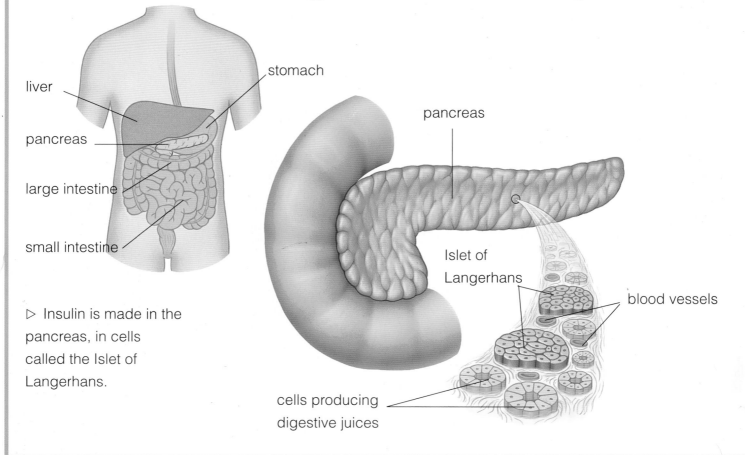

liver

stomach

pancreas

large intestine

small intestine

pancreas

Islet of Langerhans

blood vessels

cells producing digestive juices

▷ Insulin is made in the pancreas, in cells called the Islet of Langerhans.

There are several types of diabetes. Julie, Tim, and Charlie have the kind that is the most common in children—type 1 diabetes. When they were very young, the pancreas stopped making insulin. No one really knows why this happens. Without any insulin, these children cannot get energy from the food they eat. Instead, all the sugar in their food stays in their blood.

△ Type 2 diabetes tends to start in older people.

Mr. Hussain has type 2 diabetes. His pancreas can still make insulin, but the rest of his body cannot use it very well. The result is the same as with type 1 diabetes—there is too much sugar in the blood.

Diabetes tends to run in families. Scientists believe that many people who cannot make or use insulin properly inherit the problem from their parents. Getting diabetes is no one's fault, and it is not contagious.

▷ Like hair color and height, diabetes tends to run in families.

Treating Diabetes

Without treatment, people with type 1 diabetes may feel very sick. They lose weight and become weak and tired because they cannot get any energy from their food. Before doctors found out how to treat the problem, people with diabetes eventually became unconscious and died.

Now, treatment is very effective. People who do not make any insulin, such as Julie, Tim, and Charlie, can have insulin injections. Insulin always has to be injected. If you swallow insulin, it will be broken down in the stomach before it has a chance to work.

▷ Without treatment, people with diabetes feel very thirsty, drink lots of fluids, and have to urinate often.

◁ A doctor doing a simple blood test to discover whether a patient has diabetes

▽ A nurse showing a girl how to give herself an insulin injection in her thigh

People with type 2 diabetes, like Mr. Hussain, do not usually take insulin at first because the pancreas can still make it. Some people can control their sugar levels just by eating a healthful diet and exercising. Many have to take pills to control their sugar levels. People with type 2 diabetes usually have insulin injections only if other treatments do not work.

It is very important that people take their medicine every day. If they don't, they will feel sick, and as they get older, they may have problems with their eyes, their feet, or their kidneys.

Julie's Day

Every morning, Julie has to get up in plenty of time to get ready for school. She needs to have her first insulin injection of the day about half an hour before breakfast. The insulin needs to be in her blood waiting to help her body use the energy in her breakfast cereal.

People who have type 1 diabetes don't usually choose to give themselves an injection every time they eat something. It wouldn't always be easy to have lots of injections every day! Instead, Julie has two injections each day—one before breakfast and the second in the evening. Some people inject more often.

▽ Julie finds it more comfortable to give herself injections into a fatty part like her thigh.

△ When she has had her injection, Julie is ready for her meal.

△ Julie and her friends use up lots of energy during their gym classes.

Not a problem!

"Some people feel sorry for me because I have to give myself injections. But I am used to it now and I don't mind. At first, Mom or Dad used to help but now I do the shots on my own."

The insulin Julie has injected works all day long. This means that she needs to have all her meals on time. Sometimes she eats extra snacks between meals, so that the insulin has something to work on. If Julie forgets to have one snack in the morning and one in the afternoon, she may end up with too little sugar in her blood. This makes her feel shaky or dizzy, as Tim did on the bus. Julie also eats something extra before a gym class, because she needs extra energy to do her exercises.

Food and Diabetes

Take a look at the meal in the picture below. Think about what is in each dish. Which items do you think contain a lot of sugar? Which of these foods do you think someone with diabetes can eat?

The picture on the right shows the sort of meal that a person with diabetes might eat. It is surprisingly similar to the first picture. A person with diabetes could eat all the foods shown in the first picture. The main difference is that diabetics should eat smaller portions of some foods and larger amounts of others.

◁ This meal is high in fat and sugar.

◁ Although this is similar to the meal in the picture opposite, it contains less fat and sugar.

There is no reason someone with diabetes should not eat foods that contain sugar or fat, such as cookies, potato chips, or pastries. But diabetics should try to eat less of these foods and choose low-fat, low-sugar snacks instead. People with diabetes can eat french fries, but it would be more healthful to eat baked or mashed potatoes instead. Carbonated drinks are okay, but diabetics should choose sugar-free brands.

People with diabetes need to control their weight and may also have heart problems. A diet that is high in fat can make you put on weight and can be bad for your heart. If you have diabetes, you need to make sure that you do not eat too many sweet and fatty foods.

A Healthful Diet

It is important that everyone should eat a healthful, balanced diet. Most people eat too much fat and sugar. Instead of sugary, fatty snacks, it is better to eat starchy foods like bread, pasta, and potatoes. Fruit is a healthful snack to eat between meals and has plenty of fiber to help digestion. Baked beans, peas, and lentils also contain lots of fiber.

Look again at the picture on page 13. You will see that a healthful diet for a person with diabetes is very similar to the diet that everyone should try to eat in order to stay healthy. As you can see, this doesn't mean you have to cut out all your favorite foods.

▷ These foods are high in starch and fiber, but low in sugar and fat.

◁ For a healthful diet, you should aim to eat at least five helpings of fruit and vegetables every day.

▽ If you read labels, you can find out which foods are best for a healthful diet.

It is getting easier to find out how much fat, protein, sugar, vitamins, and minerals are in our food. Most food labels now show this information, which helps us plan a healthful diet.

Mr. Hussain Wants to Fast

The Hussains are Muslims. Jemilla is going to the hospital with her grandfather to talk to the nurse about fasting during Ramadan. Ramadan is the ninth month in the Muslim calendar, and, for about a month, Muslim adults fast between sunrise and sunset. During that time, they do not eat or drink. Instead, they eat two large meals a day, one just before sunrise and the other soon after sunset. These meals often contain a lot of fat and sugar to give people energy for the long fast.

Fasting is a challenge for people with diabetes because they need to eat at regular times, often with snacks between meals. With planning, however, special needs such as fasting can be met.

▷ The nurse advised Mr. Hussain not to eat too many sweet things during the two meals he has on each day of Ramadan.

A healthier diet

"My grandfather used to eat rich curries, but when he found he had diabetes, the doctor advised him to eat less fat. Now, Mom cooks meals using leaner meat, such as chicken, and just a little vegetable oil instead of animal fat. So the whole family has a healthier diet!"

△ When he fasted last year, Mr. Hussain felt sick. This year, he knows how to make sure he stays well.

The nurse advised Mr. Hussain to change the dose and timing of his pills while he fasts. It is difficult to adapt insulin treatment to fasting. Sometimes it is possible to change the dose. No one with diabetes should fast without talking to the doctor and working out how to avoid problems.

Learning about Diabetes

After Tim had a dizzy spell on the bus one day, his friends wanted to learn more about diabetes. Tim's teacher asked the diabetes nurse from the hospital to come and talk to the class.

The nurse explained why Tim had felt dizzy on the bus. There wasn't enough sugar in his blood because he had forgotten to have a quick snack before he played football. The name for this is hypoglycemia, or low blood sugar. People with diabetes who feel dizzy or shaky because they have hypoglycemia sometimes say they have had a "low."

▽ The nurse drew some pictures to show how the pancreas works.

I'm not different!

"At first, I didn't want people to know I have diabetes. I don't want them to treat me as if I'm different—I don't feel different! I was nervous when the nurse came to talk to the class, but I think my friends understand more about diabetes now."

▷ The nurse showed the class the glucose pills that Tim carries in case he feels dizzy.

The class talked about the kinds of snacks that Tim should eat. He needs something like a sandwich to give the insulin something to work on.

Tim keeps a package of glucose pills with him. If he has a low, the pills will quickly raise his blood sugar level.

It is very unusual for people with diabetes to become unconscious because they have too little sugar in their blood. Normally, they just feel dizzy, shaky, sweaty, or tired, like Tim. But the nurse explained to the class that if someone with diabetes collapses, they should get help immediately, by telling an adult or telephoning for an ambulance.

◁ Alan helps Tim by reminding him to eat his snacks.

Health Check

People with diabetes can't just take their medicine and hope it will keep their blood sugar under control. They have to be sure, so once or twice a day they do special tests.

Everyone with type 1 diabetes and some people with type 2 diabetes test a drop of their blood. They prick their finger and put the blood on a plastic strip. Some strips fit into a small, handheld machine, which shows how much sugar is in the blood. Other strips change color to show blood sugar level.

A test before breakfast and one before the evening meal show how well the insulin is working. But sometimes people with diabetes need to measure their blood sugar levels during the day.

◁ This girl is checking her blood sugar level by doing a simple blood test.

If there is too much or too little sugar in their blood, the doctor or nurse can show diabetics how to change the amount of insulin or tablets they take. They may also have to think more carefully about what they eat.

People with type 2 diabetes can check how well their medicines are working by testing the amount of sugar in their blood. This can be done with the strip method, although many people use measuring meters.

△ Once his doctor has explained how to do tests, this boy will soon feel in control of his diabetes.

Gadgets and Gizmos

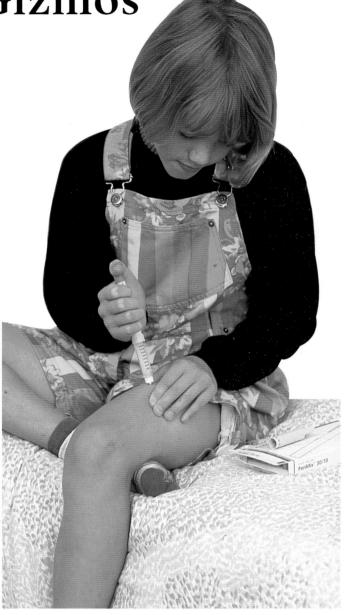

Injecting insulin gets easier all the time. Some people use an ordinary syringe but many use a syringe that looks like a small pen. They insert a tiny container of insulin into it. When they press the blunt end of the pen, it injects insulin through the skin. It is simple to use.

Instead of injecting themselves with a syringe, a few people choose to wear a small device that they can set to inject insulin at certain times. They wear the device all the time. It has a small control box attached to a needle that is in the person's skin.

▷ A small insulin pump like this gives injections at the times set by the person wearing it.

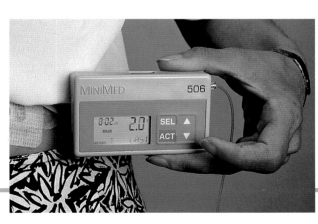

△ Some people prefer to use an insulin pen like this because it is easier to use than a syringe.

▽ People with diabetes make sure they stay healthy by having regular medical check-ups.

At least once a year, people with diabetes should have health check-ups. This often includes blood tests and checks on their eyes, nerves, and kidneys. There are usually special doctors and nurses who are used to treating diabetes and know all about it. They can help sort out any problems.

A Family Matter

Mai was fed up. Just when she needed her father to help her with her homework, he was helping Charlie to test his blood for sugar.

"It's always the same," grumbled Mai. "Charlie gets all the attention and nobody cares about me!"

△ Dad wanted to see the result of Charlie's blood test, but Mai was feeling left out.

"You know that's not true," said her father. "I came to watch you in the school play yesterday instead of going to Charlie's baseball game."

Dad sat down with Mai and Charlie. Both children know a lot about diabetes already. They understand what causes it and why Charlie needs insulin injections. Mai tries not to eat candy in front of Charlie because she knows he cannot have them as often as she can.

"Sometimes, Charlie's diabetes has to come first," said Dad. "He needs to test his blood every day and have his injections on time, otherwise he might be sick."

"I know," said Mai. "But it always seems to be when I need you too."

△ Mai and Charlie both felt better after their talk with Dad.

Dad laughed. "It only takes a few minutes to help Charlie, and there's plenty of time to help you too."

"I do most of my injections and tests on my own now, so I won't need that much help," said Charlie.

"That's right, and then we can both help Mai with her homework," said Dad.

Mai made a face and said, "If Charlie tries to help, I'm sure to get it all wrong!"

Will Diabetes Ever Go Away?

Scientists are trying to learn more about diabetes. They want to improve treatment so that people don't develop problems with their eyes, feet, heart, kidneys, and nerves. Doctors are studying the way people can inherit diabetes from their parents. They hope to find a way to prevent both types of diabetes. Another aim is to find a way to give a person with diabetes a new pancreas. Doctors can transplant organs like the kidney and heart, but transplanting a pancreas is more difficult.

▽ Scientists are trying to find out how diabetes is passed on from parents to children.

It may be many years before scientists find a way to prevent diabetes. But there are lots of things you can do to protect yourself from getting type 2 diabetes when you are older.

▷ Make exercise a part of your life and stay fit.

▽ Because they can develop foot problems, people with diabetes need to look after their feet.

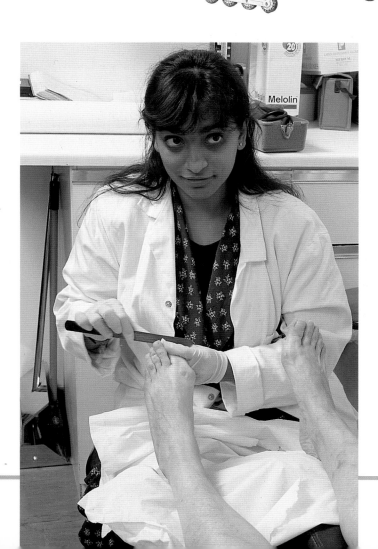

Adults are more likely to get diabetes if they are overweight. By eating a healthful diet and getting plenty of exercise now, you can help make sure that you will be healthier later in life.

Nobody wants to have diabetes. But you've seen that Julie, Tim, Charlie, and Mr. Hussain all lead normal, active lives. They don't let their diabetes get in the way. You don't need to feel sorry for people with diabetes or act differently around them.

Getting Help

People who have diabetes get to know the doctors and nurses who look after them. They usually need the most help when they first discover that they have diabetes. It takes a while to get used to checking your blood sugar, taking your insulin or other medicine, and planning a healthful diet.

In most countries, there are special organizations for people with diabetes. They bring together groups of people with diabetes and their families. It is good to talk to other people who have diabetes. They may have had similar problems and experiences and might have some useful ideas about how to cope.

△ A group of people with type 2 diabetes meet to talk and give each other support.

Most hospitals have information about diabetes and its treatment.

The American Diabetes Association also provides plenty of information for people of all ages about diabetes, blood sugar testing, meal planning, insulin, and much more.

▷ These young people are on a camping trip organized by a support group for people with diabetes.

Children with diabetes can go on family outings and school trips that other children enjoy. But sometimes it is good for them to meet others where everyone has diabetes, to share experiences, and to gain confidence. Groups like the ADA organize activities to help children meet and have a good time.

The more you know about diabetes and how to look after it, the less scary it is.

Glossary

Blood A liquid that flows all around the body, carrying oxygen and protein, fat, and sugar from our food.

Cell All living things are made up of millions of tiny parts, called cells. Groups of millions of cells form organs like the pancreas.

Digestion The process by which the body breaks down food and turns it into energy and waste products.

Dose A carefully worked-out amount of medication.

Fast To go without food (and sometimes drink).

Fat Part of our food that gives us energy. Eating too much fat is not healthy.

Fiber A part of food that helps keep the intestine healthy.

Gland A small part of the body that produces chemicals, such as insulin.

Hypoglycemia Lower than normal levels of sugar in the blood.

Inherit To be born with a physical problem or feature that has been passed on from the body of a parent.

Insulin A chemical made by the pancreas that controls sugar levels in the body.

Intestine A long tube that is part of the system that digests food.

Kidneys Organs in the lower part of the body that process body waste and produce urine.

Mineral A natural substance found in some foods, which is needed to keep the body healthy.

Nerve A thin fiber that passes messages around the body.

Pancreas The gland that makes insulin and other chemicals needed for digestion.

Protein An important part of our food that is needed for growth, to repair damaged parts of the body, and to fight infection.

Ramadan A period of fasting carried out by adult Muslims. It is one of the most important requirements of the Islamic religion.

Syringe A small plastic or glass tube with a needle at one end. A syringe is used to inject substances into the body through the skin.

Transplant To move a healthy organ from one body to another body. To replace an organ that no longer works properly.

Urine A waste fluid produced by the kidneys.

Vitamin A natural substance found in some foods, which is needed to keep the body healthy.

Further Information

Ferber, Elizabeth. *Diabetes* (Millbrook Medical Library). Brookfield, CT: Millbrook Press, 1996.

Kelly, Pat. *Diabetes* (Coping Library). New York: Rosen Group, 1998.

Landau, Elaine. *Diabetes* (Understanding Illness). New York: 21st Century Books, 1995.

Mirsky, Stanley and Heilman, Joan. *Controlling Diabetes the Easy Way*. New York: Random House, 1985.

Semple, Carol McCormick. *Diabetes* (Healthwatch). Parsippany, NJ: Crestwood House, 1995.

Silverstein, Alvin. *Diabetes* (Diseases and People). Springfield, NJ: Enslow Publishing, 1994.

Your local doctor's office or hospital will be able to provide you with information about diabetes and its treatment.

There are many Internet sites about diabetes. The following are designed for children:

- http://www.castleweb.com/diabetes.
  Produced by Children with Diabetes, this site gives access to information, groups and penpals.

- http://www.diabetes.com/site.
  The American Diabetes Association web site. Look for Kool Kids.

- http://www.diabetes.org
  The American Diabetes Association web site.

- http://www.geocities.com/HotSprings/6935/index.html.
  A site for children who want to learn about diabetes.

- http://www.thehumanelement.com/courage/.
  Cartoons about Courage, the superhero who has diabetes.

Index